Imagine the Future...

A Teenager's Guide to the 21st Century....
and Beyond

Today's success came from yesterday's learning. Tomorrow's success will come from what we learn today.

We know what we are, but know not what we may be.

Shakespeare

ISBN:0-9655806-0-1

Table of Contents

Fastest growing occupations

Fastest growing industries

Industries with largest job growth

Reasons to go to college

Reasons why *not* to go to college

Reasons why people chose the college they did

College credits through CLEP

External Degree Programs

Median starting salaries of college grads, 1993

The military option

Recommended reading list

Preface

When you're ready

One evening, after listening to a set of motivational tapes in my car, I came home and quickly wrote the word ATTITUDE in bright red, capital letters on two pieces of heavy, white paper. I showed them to my sons, Chris and Aaron, telling them that this was the secret to success and went into a long explanation. Then I put one sign on each of the bathroom mirrors. Over time, the moisture corroded the signs and they were discarded.

About three years later, Christian came home from a week-end of martial arts training and proceeded to put three signs on the bathroom mirror. They read: ATTITUDE , DO NOT KID YOURSELF TODAY and DISCIPLINE HURTS LESS THAN REGRET. I was surprised to see such powerful statements posted, so I went to him and said, "When I put the ATTITUDE sign up and talked with you about it, it seemed to have no impact. What happened?"
He looked at me and said, simply, "I wasn't ready."

Perhaps you would say the same to me about this book. I would understand. But I would still ask you to trust me and read it anyway, because what's in this book is like a seed. You may not give it your full undivided attention now, but the seed will be planted and, over time it will grow and come to mean something — when you are ready.

You may not be thinking about school or your future right now. You may be more concerned with who to invite to the movies or what to wear. At some point, as you move closer to the day that you will leave school, some of what you read here will help you — perhaps, by reminding you to reflect on what's important to you — perhaps in how you start to think about your next moves. You might even re-read parts of this book again. When you are ready, it'll be there. After all, the big changes in your life are only a couple years away.

Looking Forward

There are more exciting opportunities in the world today than ever before. There is also greater risk than we have faced in three generations. Fewer people in the U.S. today have the skills and abilities needed to fill the requirements of the workplace of the future. As a result, employers are forced to respond by either going off-shore, sending the jobs where there are skills to match, or seeking immigrants with the necessary training and skills and bringing them to the U.S. At the same time, increasing numbers of educated people around the world are entering the work force with the express intent of creating a good life for themselves and their families.

You can take advantage of this situation if you absorb the knowledge and hone the skills that will be in demand. Or, you can accept mediocrity and suffer the consequences. Few are up to the challenge. How about you?

This book is written for you, a teenager who is thoughtfully making decisions about your own future and is looking for some guidance. What I've compiled here is information about jobs, a description of how work will be structured when you arrive on the scene, who you'll be competing with, and what's in it for you. I've also given you food for thought that can help you as you think about what you'd like to experience in your life: work you'd like to do, fun you'd like to have, adventures you'd like to live.

You'll find this book is:

- *Fun to read*, filled with good information.
- *Organized* to provide a clear overview of the opportunities, risks, and the requirements for success, including how to get *legitimate* external college degrees.
- *Flexible*. You don't have to read it from cover-to-cover if you want "just the facts."

There are only seven chapters, each developed along the lines of the seminars I've created for teens like you. Each chapter discusses a different area of importance to you. At the end of each chapter I've summarized for you what I think is most important. The summary is titled *If we were together I would emphasize*. Following the summary is a blank section titled *Action Plans*. This space is for you to write in your personal action commitments. It may be as simple as committing to read a book from the recommended list or to talk with someone about something you read. In any case, as you reach the end of a chapter, ask yourself "What can I do with what I've learned?" Then, commit to do it.

Your responsibilities

Great ideas are imagined every day by all sorts of people. However, most of them never become reality because the dreamer never took action. You can wish all you want about things that you'd like to have or do or be, but without actions your dreams will never be realized. My friend, your success or failure lies in *Action* or inaction — you decide which.

When I point out opportunities for you to consider, I am constrained by time and space. So, I'll provide an overview to give you a sense of the topic and provide you with the names of the best books to read. It will then be up to you to decide how you want to proceed (*Action* or inaction). I'll do my part; you do yours. Your willingness to jump in to improve yourself is a mark of your maturity. I'm sure you'll meet the challenge.

A separate book accompanies this one. It was written for your parents, specifically so they would have some inkling of what we are sharing so that they might support you on your journey to adulthood and in your life after high school. The intent was to give you the chance to open up a dialogue with your parents about your vision for your future, your goals, fears and aspirations. It's rare that someone your age is crystal clear about his or her future and has mapped out a complete strategy to reach it. You'll need help from your folks and others to clarify where you want to go, the path you want to take and how you're going to get there.

Take advantage of this book as an opportunity to open the conversation with your parents if, for whatever reason, they don't initiate it first.

Soon you will be going out on your own, to take wing and soar with the eagles. Even so, you'll probably always cherish the links to your family. The strength of the bond you form and reinforce now can last a lifetime for you all. Build a bridge - extend a hand.

Introduction

An important lesson learned

Imagine a quiet street of look-alike houses in a small suburban town. I remember standing in my friend Jack's office in his small three bedroom ranch, looking out the window at the street. I was angry with my father, who lived in Italy and worked as a civil servant for the U.S. Government. Once again, he was late with the check that held us together month - to - month. I was angry because my mother had to work at the local W. T. Grant department store for $1 an hour to make ends meet. I was angry because there were things I couldn't do and things I couldn't have that other kids in my town could afford.

Jack listened quietly as I spewed venom about my Dad. He listened with the patience of the thoughtful parent he had become from raising his own children. When he did speak, what he said changed my life.

" I'm really moved by your story. I'm sure that if you told this to other people, they would be moved, too. It's a sad story. But I have to caution you. There's one thing you should never do. You should never start to believe your own bullshit.

I know that what you're saying is true. You don't have things the way you want. But whatever you become, and whatever you will make of your life is up to you, not what your dad did or didn't do. In the final analysis, your choices, your decisions and your actions will determine the quality of your life, and no one else's."

In *your* final analysis, the same lesson holds true for you. What you become and the quality of your life is up to you. It is up to you to decide: what you want to do with your life; what you want your life to be like; what you want it to mean; the actions you will take to make your life unfold as you wish.

The life you will lead is unique to you. It is not your parents' path, or anyone else's. It is yours. So you must decide what shape it will take, what outcomes it will fulfill. Think it through. Make it true to you.

Prepare yourself in every way

It is not so important at your age that you have a clear vision of what you want to be. What is important is that when you do decide, that *no one* will be able to prevent you from being it.

The ability to do what *you* want to do only comes from preparation. If you decide someday that you want to be a doctor, yet you have no foundation in the essential sciences (biology, chemistry, anatomy, physiology), you're stopped. If you decide someday that you want to be a lawyer, yet you are not versed in required skills (English, communication skills, critical and creative thinking), you're stopped.

Whenever you decide what you want to be, if you're not versed in the basics, you're stopped; and the one who has stopped you is *you!*

These are the years you give to your preparation, though for what may be unclear. Don't worry about it. Worry about the *process* of preparing — and preparing well. Consider your personal interests and your personal

14

strengths and build on them. Invest your time in developing and honing your thinking, analytical, language and communication skills. Functional skills, like accounting, engineering or marketing can be learned later - and better - *after* you've developed your critical thinking processes.

Take on the toughest classes consistent with your abilities and do your best in them. Grades are not as important as the effort you put in and the depth of your learning. If you get a *B* or *C* in a difficult class, but know in your mind that you gave it your best, accept the grade with pride and move on to the next challenges.

Here is a lesson about grades that I learned from my son, Aaron. Following his acceptance to Oakland University Honors College (HC), Aaron experienced first-hand the art of learning at a higher level. His first honors class, simply titled *The Second Time Around*, required him to read fourteen books!

While Aaron found his three regular classes were reasonably easy, the HC course was bewildering. " I don't even know what the professor is talking about half the time. And it's strange, because most of the rest of the students do, and they're talking up a storm."

Aaron's first insight into what he was missing came when he received his first paper back. The grade was a *C*, with the following notation: "You did a great job of telling me what the author was saying. I know what he was saying. What I want to know is what *you* think about it."

After that everything went smoothly, and there was an obvious change in Aaron. He said, "I finally caught on. Now I'm one of the best contributors in the class - and it's great fun. But, I'm afraid that, because there are very few assignments in the course, my grade will still be around a *C*." It was. The grades in his other classes were between 3.8 and 4.0, but his first semester grade point average (GPA) was 3.4. I was impressed and pleased by his wisdom, however, when he said, looking at his grades, "The HC course cost me about .4 points, but it was worth the price to learn how to think for myself." Sometimes the transition to a new level of accomplishment has an unexpected price. Pay it.

1 —The World You Will Enter

In the future that is unfolding, approximately 91 percent of all work done in the United States will be in the information and service industries. Manufacturing will account for some 5 percent, and only about 4 percent will be in mining and farming.

Manufacturing   Mining & Agriculture

Information & Services

Here's what it means for you. Brawn will be replaced by brain. What you know and who you know will matter more than physical prowess and stamina.

In the future that is unfolding, almost half of us will be self-employed, and about a third of us will be working in small to medium sized companies. Fewer than one out of five of us will have traditional careers with the large, multinational companies.

Large Corporations

Self-emplo

Small - Medium Size Firms

Here's what it means for you. You will have any number of jobs, and as many as three to four careers. You'll be an independent agent for a large part of your career, so you'll have to learn to be self sufficient, networking to get jobs, balancing your income to carry yourself over lean times. This isn't all bad. If your skills are in demand and if you market them well, you'll find plenty of work. The key is to stay ahead of the trends and change with the times.

Working independently is not new in this country or the world. Billions of people are self-employed (not unemployed). One characteristic of being an independent that you must develop, cherish and protect is your reputation and honor. The concept of closing a deal with a handshake instead of signing a multi-page contract will return because it is simply expedient. In some parts of the world, this is the way it has been for decades, even centuries. It is that way in the jewelry trade throughout the world. It is that way in the jewelry trade in New York City.

Walk along 47th Street in Manhattan, and you will almost invariably see diamond traders making trades right on the street. A buyer will look through his magnifying glass to determine the quality of the diamonds he is considering. If he and the seller reach an agreement, diamonds and cash trade hands. A deal is consummated. In this part of the city, reputation is so valued, that if a person is shown to be underhanded or an outright crook, *no one* in the trade will do business with him *ever* again. It has been that way for centuries. It is that way today. When you start in your career, you will be accorded honor. Lose it, and you'd better find another career.

In the past, the fate of individuals was tied largely to the fate of our large companies. Today, most large and medium companies are global and use resources globally. In the economy of the future, the fates of individuals will rest with themselves. The knowledge they have and the value they create will determine their success. Because we are a part of the global economy, we must compete on that basis. This includes the high tech and information segments of our business, where many feel we have the edge. In fact, we do have a slight advantage, but it is fading fast.

Retaining an edge is a personal survival tactic. Not everyone will do equally well, and some won't make it. In reality, life has always been a competition from which some return victorious while others are vanquished. The well-known historians, Will and Ariel Durant put it this way in their book, *The Lessons of History* :

"In the competition for food or mates or power some organisms succeed and some fail. In the struggle for existence some individuals are better equipped than others to meet the tests of survival. Since Nature (here meaning total reality and its processes) has not read very carefully the American Declaration of Independence or the French Revolutionary Declaration of the Rights of Man, we are all born unfree and unequal: subject to our physical and psychological heredity, and to the customs and traditions of our group; diversely endowed in health and strength, in mental capacity and qualities of character. Nature loves difference as the necessary material of selection and evolution; identical twins differ in a hundred ways, and no two peas are alike." [1]

Here's what it means for you. Your skills will be tested against people from around the world. If your skills are good and you are actively caring for your career, you have a good chance at having a better than average life style whether you market your skills locally or globally. For more on this, see Chapter 6 - Personal Issues.

Many totally new and exciting industries are unfolding that will afford new opportunities for people with the skills and attitudes to perform them. These industries include: aerospace, virtual reality, interactive television, mechatronics, robotics, biotechnology, artificial intelligence, environmental technology, and genetic engineering, to name a few. While these may seem like industries that are common, uncommon, explosive changes are unfolding within them.

- In aerospace for example, countries are working together to launch satellites from portable oil rigs. This will allow the missiles to be transported to and launched from the equator, where they have the advantage of gaining momentum from the earth's rotation.

- Hypertext is creating a whole new way of communicating by allowing readers to connect to other sites. Unlike a story written in a book, literary works in hypertext can have no beginning, middle or end. Readers just jump in and make their own paths through the stories. They can make personal choices on where they want to go because there are no boundaries. Imagine what that must be like.

New technology will change or eliminate many old-line industries, and jobs in those industries will decline or die out. Many jobs will be *de-skilled,* that is, made so much easier to do that people with lower skills will be able to do them — at substantially lower wages. Two examples of this are the job of cashiers and the supposedly high tech job of electrocardiogram (EKG) technicians who work in hospitals and doctors' offices. New cash registers, using both scanners and icon buttons (with pictures) have lowered the required skills of cashiers. Many companies have dropped their job requirements for math skills and, with the reduction in skills, they've lowered the wages they pay. Technicians who once assisted doctors in using specialized equipment to graph patients' heart performance are virtually out of a job. Today, EKG machines not only monitor and graph heart performance, they make diagnoses. Any lower level employee can hook the patient up to the machine. This job category is about the only one in the growing medical field that has negative job growth in its forecast. It won't be alone for long.

Increasingly, companies are creating expert systems that take people out of the process, making it faster, easier and cheaper to do just about anything. Think of your last credit card purchase. The cashier ran your card through a magnetic scanner and, almost instantly, the machine issued an approval number. This process used to take a lot longer when the cashier had to call in for approval, read the credit card number to a person on the other end of the line, and wait for approval. That job no longer exists in over 99 percent of the transactions today.

Credit approval without human involvement

is faster, easier, and less painful for customers — and less expensive for the company.

Can you think of any functions that are done better, faster, easier and cheaper through technology? Sure you can. That's why it is so important that you stay ahead of changes in technology with applicable skills and why you should remain ever vigilant in looking for new problems to solve.

Here's what it means for you. You should invest your time in learning how to think, evaluate and assess. The actual doing of things can be done by anyone. Look at who will be doing well in the new environment. Agriculture specialists who help other countries grow the food their people will need. Bankers who will help the countries set up financial systems they need to run their countries. Engineers with the skills to help others build roads, dams other parts of a country's infrastructure. They are all consultants. Musicians, scriptwriters (English skills), actors, film makers, scientists with specific knowledge, martial arts masters, choreographers. Everyone has knowledge, a skill or a talent that is needed and valued by others. You can develop your skills and talents, too. And, you can be doing work that you enjoy.

In the future, the fastest growing opportunities for many old-line industries will be in the developing nations. Our markets for cars, appliances, hand tools are pretty much tapped. In emerging nations, there are billions of people who have none of what we have — and they want it.

Most U.S. companies are looking at the emerging nations as their next opportunities. Pepsi and Coca Cola see millions of cola deprived mouths for their soft drinks, and plenty of mouths for Kentucky Fried Chicken or Tacos. They will send managers to fill many spots throughout the world until they can develop home-grown managers.

Parlez-vous Francais?

Habla Ud. Español?

If you can respond to questions like these with a YES, you'll have an advantage in the new economy.

What skills do you think they want their managers to have? Sure, finance and accounting are important. What about language and interpersonal skills, and cultural sensitivity? What about team building and leadership skills? You bet! How long will a manager work in another country? Five to ten years! Would you like the challenge of running a business in another country? How are your skills?

The case for lifelong learning

Not long ago a person could get through life with what little he or she had learned by the eighth grade. Many people believe it is still this way. Occasionally I'll hear graduates say, "I'm glad school is finally over. I'll never read another book as long as I live." And they mean it!

This can't be the case for you. Because changes are happening so fast, it is imperative that you stay ahead of the curve just to do well. You must look at lifelong learning now as an investment in yourself. It's no longer a luxury. Lifelong learning is necessary for survival.

As you will read later (see Competition), India made major investments in some of its people and has created an industry base that is prized by global industries, including Texas

Instruments, Oracle, Hewlett-Packard. The result is good paying jobs and an increase in the local standard of living for its best people.

It is important for you to know that companies in many other countries actively train both their new hires and long time employees. They do this to insure that their *industry* will always have a good supply of qualified workers. The companies acknowledge that they might lose employees they have trained to a competitor. They also know that they can hire others away from their competition. Their mutual goal is to make sure that there are enough quality prospects to go around, regardless of who trained them.

Training in the United States is not based on such an enlightened understanding. U.S. companies invest very little in training their employees, so if they lose one to the competition, they haven't lost so much. On the other hand, when they entice workers away, they are not getting much either. The real losers are the companies as a group. They have to compete with global workers who have received the benefits of training.

A number of comparisons have been included in the appendix that reinforce this message: *If you are going to stay abreast or ahead of changes, commit to rely on yourself.* Your company won't do it for you. The reason for you to do it is that continuous personal growth is also continuous added value. It is what makes you worthy of being employed.

Look at these comparisons: In Japan, between 58 and 90% of employees receive formal training, depending on the size of the company. The larger the company, the larger the percentage. In the U.S., the numbers range from under 10% to just over 23%.[2]

In Japan, almost 80% of employees receive training starting at the first year and continuing through their working lives with the company. These people are always current in the latest methods of work.

In the U.S., less than 10% of new employees receive formal training. The numbers don't reach 20% until employees have been on the job for 6 years or more. Further, not all workers get trained. The people who get the most training are in management or technical areas: those getting the least are laborers, clerical sales, and service providers. Do you think there's a relationship between those who get the training (investment) and their respective salaries?

Similar comparisons hold true of France, Germany and other industrialized nations. Germany is noted for its apprenticeship programs. Graduates from these intense programs can earn upwards of $70 thousand per year without a college degree. They bring much needed and prized skills to the workplace and are rewarded for them.

With the accelerated pace of change, if you have not kept current with advances for six years, you'll be a dinosaur and at risk of losing your job. If you are self-employed, you'll probably have lost most of your clients.

If we were together, I would emphasize

Action Steps

* You are responsible for keeping up.

* Invest in yourself even if you have to pay

Action Steps

your own money.

* Staying abreast of changes affords you an opportunity to participate in those changes and be rewarded for your efforts.

* Personal growth is portable.

1. Will & Ariel Durant,*The Lessons of History*, New York, Simon & Schuster, p.19

2. American Society for Training and Development

2 — Job Opportunities

In the appendix you will be exposed to a wide variety of job opportunities that are unfolding in two to eight years as projected by the Bureau of Labor Statistics. The agency lists over 250 separate categories of occupations, from executives to waiters and waitresses. I've provided descriptions on the categories with the largest numbers of job openings and the fastest growing industries. In addition, there is a chart that reports the earnings of recent college graduates by sex and by major field of study.

It is estimated that over half the jobs that will become available in your working lifetime have yet to be created. This makes sense when you consider the number of changes occurring right now and the pace of those changes. Jobs like web page designers and video game software developers were unheard of just a few years ago. More and more, as new areas of endeavor (from communication to biotechnology to space travel) open up or expand, they will require enhanced or totally new skills, new languages and new ways of thinking.

At this stage of your life you should look at all the types of work that interest you. In fact, it makes good sense to take the broad view. But, don't just make a list of job names. Imagine for thirty seconds that you <u>are</u> the person doing that job. Try to get the sense and feel of it. Is it comfortable? How do you feel doing it? What are you experiencing? What are the skills needed to do the job well? At your leisure, go on to another job and try it on.

For best results, make a record of your thoughts and feelings about each job and of the skills you've identified. Then compare the list you've made to a published list of requirements for the job, which you can get from your career counselor, the local library or the Bureau of Labor Statistics.

If you've considered a number of jobs, look for similarities in the skills required. You'll be amazed at how many skills are *common* to numerous unrelated fields. For example, interpersonal skills (the ability to get along with and influence others), communication skills (the ability to organize thoughts and have others understand them) are essential skills that apply to almost all human interaction. They are as applicable in an engineering office as they are at an accounting firm or the NASA space agency. Ask yourself, "Knowing what I know now, how will I approach the courses I am taking in school?"

Let's start with the sciences.

Medicine - Within this field lies the need for *researchers* to uncover cures for diseases that afflict great numbers of people - from Alzheimer's, which slowly attacks a person's mind until he or she no longer has a memory, to AIDS, which is decimating societies, especially in Asia and Africa. Imagine that you are part of the team that solves one major mystery. How would you feel knowing that your contribution would impact millions of people all over the world?

There are *plastic surgeons* who leave their practices once a year and spend time in out-of-the way villages in impoverished countries and use their talents to reconstruct the scarred faces of children. Imagine you are the doctor who repaired a child's cleft lip and freed her to live a normal life, free from ridicule. Think of the burden you would lift from both her and her parents, and the gratitude they would express. How would you feel about giving those gifts?

Demand is even greater for registered nurses, medical assistants, home health aides and nursing aides. This group will account for 1.6 million new jobs out of the expected 2.7 million new jobs for health occupations as a whole. The aging of America will offer great jobs for the life of your career.

There are others, from pediatricians to heart and lung specialists to neurosurgeons. Think about them, research their work, ask yourself, "What if...?"

Engineering - You are exposed to the work of engineers in every facet of your life. Design engineers were instrumental in bringing us innovations in everything from cars to refrigerators to furniture and the fasteners that hold them together. We would not be flying, driving or even riding bicycles but for the ideas of engineers. Chemical engineers gave us the memory in the hard disk drive, durable automobiles and washing machines, the circuit boards that fill everything from cars to televisions (which are *designed* by electrical engineers). The Olympic Village in Atlanta was constructed of composite materials with the strength of steel and the lightness of plastic. The entire village was designed to be collapsed onto truck beds (which were part of the construction) and sent elsewhere for reuse— including all the utilities! Much of the technology used in this project was a result of knowledge gained from the space programs.

Don't overlook the new engineering fields such as genetic engineering, biotechnology and telecommunication engineers of all types. Could you be one? The second fastest growing cluster of new jobs (engineers, natural scientists, mathematicians, systems analysts and computer scientists) will add over 1.3 million jobs through 2005.

Education

Why would you want to be a teacher? Perhaps because you have a strong need to give of yourself and to share knowledge with others, to develop minds and mold ideas. If you could mentor students to find the life that is most rewarding for them; if you could be visited by appreciative former students who came back years later to say "thanks" for all you've given them, would that be something you'd like?

Education - related occupations will add some 2 million people by 2005, both in public and private services. The jobs will vary from secondary school and special education teachers to teachers aides and counselors.

Food, Cleaning, Personal and Protective Services

Growth in the first three categories (Food, Cleaning, and Personal Services) will be faster than the average because increasing numbers of people are working and will be eating out more. They will have less time to take care of personal chores, like housekeeping, so they will hire people to do them. Growth in the travel and tourism industry is creating demands for chefs, with salaries often above $80,000 per year at upscale resorts.

Increasing concerns about safety will increase the demand for protection, from guards at apartment complexes to increased security at shopping centers. With the growth of prisons comes work for prison guards, with salaries in excess of $25,000 per year, plus benefits.

While the jobs projected are significant (over half a million), the jobs are, for the most part, low paying and have high turnover rates.

The jobs that aren't - yet

There are literally thousands of job classifications listed by the U.S. Government Department of Labor. In your lifetime you might have jobs that don't exist today. These jobs will be necessary, challenging and rewarding. Some will occur in aerospace as the country moves toward its first attempts to station people in space. Others will result from evolutionary growth and expansion in communication technologies. Still more will come in advances in medicine and biotechnology. Will you be ready? If you prepare now, and remain adaptable, the answer is yes.

Preparation comes through learning the essentials — reading, writing, math and sciences — and supplementing them with advanced learning in critical thinking skills, problem identification and problem solving skills, and systems thinking.

The key to learning these skills is balance. You don't have to do it all at once. Nor do you have to do it all. As a high school student, you have time to assess your future, to plan and lay out your objectives, to investigate and experiment, and to modify and change. Getting a solid footing in the basics gives you a solid foundation on which you can build just about anything.

Caution: As you think about the things you might like to do, understand that until you <u>try</u> them, they'll only be a "thought" or a gut feeling that has not been put to the test. Here's an example. I had a friend who always dreamed of being a nurse - until the summer she volunteered as a candy striper at the local hospital. She hated it! She didn't like the noise, the frantic pace, the smells or administering aid. She was glad she found it out early and before she committed to a career.

If we were together, I would emphasize   **Action Steps**

* Be daring and test your instincts. If you find they missed the mark, you are, in fact, ahead of the game because you eliminated one possibility and can now move ahead to test another.

* This is the time in your life to try many things. Use the time well.

* There are many things we'd like to do because, on the surface, we see them as noble or exciting or interesting. Don't base your judgments on superficial feelings. Test the concepts before you continue.

3— The Changing Structure of Work

Now let's take a look at work from another perspective, classifying work into only three large categories: *production work, in-person work,* and *knowledge work.* In large part, this comes from the writings of Robert B. Reich, Secretary of Labor in the Clinton Administration, a member of Harvard University's John F. Kennedy School of Government, and a leading political economist.

There are major differences both between and within the three categories. They include the kind of work done in each group, where the work can be done, salaries that can be expected, and the futures of each category. I urge you to read this chapter closely for it is one of the most important in the book, along with the chapter on skills. Better still, read Reich's book. It's exceptional.

Production work requires relatively low skill, is done repetitively, and in high volumes. These jobs include work like assembling cars, sewing clothes, or flipping hamburgers at a fast food restaurant. They also include data entry, like typing a manuscript, billing customers, or inputting data into insurance forms. Workers in this category don't come into contact with the end users. Their work environment is an open layout with hundreds of people doing the same types of work. Their performance is judged by their output, which is measured in units — so many wheels or shirts or invoices per hour, day, or week. Employers want people who can follow the rules, are reliable, and loyal. Educational requirements in the United States call for a high school diploma or equivalent. In most countries, there are no such requirements.

Pay can vary dramatically, depending on where the job is located and the presence or absence of a strong union. A Brazilian shoe factory worker earns only about $56 per *month*. An American worker earns more than that in a day. An auto assembly worker in a union shop in the U.S. makes a much better wage than the assembly employee in a non-union U.S. shop. An auto assembly worker at Chrysler in China earns $3,600/year; his counterpart in the U.S. can earn ten times that or more.

Taken as a whole, production workers are mostly nonwhite and female. Production work accounts for about 25 percent of all domestic workers. Production work is declining due to outsourcing and automation.

In-person work is done by people who work face-to-face with the customers who benefit from the work being done. In-person jobs include such diverse occupations as plumber, carpenter, physical therapist, taxi driver, bar tender, and hotel housekeeper. Most workers in this category come into contact with the end-user. These people usually work alone or in small groups. Employers look for people who, like production workers, are reliable, loyal, and can take orders. Since most of these employees come into contact with their clients or the company's clients, they must also be pleasant and personable.

Earnings vary widely in this group as well. Housekeepers and waitresses earn much less than physical therapists, dental hygienists, or translators.

Education levels also vary, from high school or equivalent to specialized vocational training to a Masters degree. The majority of workers in this classification, which accounts for almost a third of the labor force, are women. As you'll recall from the job projections, this category will grow very fast in the next decade.

Knowledge workers, called "symbolic analysts" by Reich, operate in just about all industries, using skills in problem identification and problem solving, conceptual thinking, and communication to provide their services across the globe. This category includes scientists, engineers, computer software creators, lawyers, real estate developers, marketing and sales professionals, writers, film producers, and musicians to name just a few.

Knowledge workers can work alone or in small groups. They can form temporary alliances for a single assignment or they can develop long-lasting associations. Knowledge workers spend most of their time on identifying opportunities (problems), and coming up with the answers (solutions). Think of movie producers, writers, and actors who collaborate on a movie and, once completed, move on to other associations. There are no lifetime contracts here. Each person is involved because his or her skills and talents *fit* the need of the moment.

If you own a computer modem, you know that inside the box it came in were the modem itself and the software to run it. Each was made by a different company. Each company warranties only its component and each mails you announcements regarding its own upgrades. Imagine how important team work is to the end result. If one company's contribution doesn't perform to standards, the company might soon disappear from existence.

Most of the population of this category are white males, although nonwhites and women are increasing in numbers and influence. Earnings vary according to the nature of the job and service provided, from tens of thousands of dollars to millions. Earnings are the best of the three categories. This group enjoys the best life styles.

Currently about twenty percent of the jobs are in this group. Growth in this area is limited, and competition will become even more intense as increasing numbers of people around the world gain the knowledge and skills to participate. Just as production work has been able to go off-shore, so has knowledge work. Many examples of this movement in jobs were cited earlier. Even so, knowledge work is where the best opportunities lie.

When you think about your place in the future world of work, balance the things you love to do with the quality of life you want to have. Often, with planning, you can have a great life doing what you love. If you'd like that, too, then try this exercise:

The road to happiness lies in two simple principles: find what it is that interests you and that you can do well, and when you find it put your whole soul into it-- every bit of energy and ambition and natural ability you have.

John D. Rockefeller III

- Draw three large circles on paper. In the first circle list all the things you love to do, regardless of how good you are at doing them. In the second, list all the things you do really well, regardless of whether you like to do them. From these two circles, select all the things you love to do and are good to great at for the final circle. You'll probably have enough things

46

in the third circle to consider as options for your future work, many of which could provide you a comfortable financial living.

When you think about the different career possibilities, look both at your passion for each and the quality of life a job in each field would provide you if you pursued it full time. If the anticipated earnings for a career you'd love to have are satisfactory to you, put a check next to it and go on to evaluate another. You may have many more than one. If the career you find most desirable won't sustain the life style you need, you've got a decision to make. One option is to consider a different job that you find challenging and rewarding personally, and that can satisfy your financial needs as well. Then you can pursue your primary passion as an avocation or hobby.

There are many starving artists striving for their day of recognition. You may elect to be one of them, saying, in effect, "forget the conventional life. I'm going to do what I need to do, what I feel I must do. I'm willing to do whatever it takes to fulfill my dream. I'm willing to forego comforts if necessary." If

Life is to be lived. If you have to support yourself, you had bloody well better find some way that is going to be interesting. And you don't do that by sitting around wondering about yourself.

Katharine Hepburn

Starting out to make money is the greatest mistake in life. Do what you feel you have a flair for doing, and if you are good enough at it, the money will come.

Greer Garson

47

that is your choice, just be sure that you've thought it through. That being said, go for it. Not everyone starves.

An example is René, a graphic designer of good repute. She works with a number of large advertising agencies and marketing companies as well as a number of smaller companies that can't afford to use ad agencies. Her strengths lie in her natural ability to understand what clients need and to work with them to achieve it, whether its a large campaign or a simple brochure. She works with other independents who write the text or print the brochures.

In a similar fashion, my friend, Leonard, is an expert at locating new and used medical equipment. His reputation is global. People call on him to find equipment for them. Leonard is an independent problem solver— very good and very handsomely rewarded for his knowledge.

Both René and Leonard value their independence. René really likes working with a number of different colleagues on a variety of challenges. Leonard values money, lots of it. It buys him freedom. As the money comes in, he invests it in condos or stocks or whatever he thinks will be the best use of the money at the moment. Both see their best investment is in themselves.

Action Steps   **If we were together, I would emphasize**

* Look closely at the areas that hold your most passionate interests. Look seriously at the economic prospects they offer. If they cannot sustain one person, let alone two or a family, ask yourself whether you can afford them in your life. Poverty <u>is</u> everything it's cracked up to be.

* If you knowingly want to follow a dream, even though it offers little financial reward, that is your choice.

* Life is finite. Follow the dream of your choice.

* Life is also a balancing act. If others will be a part of your life, you must factor them into your decisions.

4 — Skills You Will Need

The global gap in skills has been narrowing for decades. It will narrow within your working life until we are equal with other nations. As a result, you will see their wages go up as yours decline until we achieve a form of global *leveling* of incomes. Currently, what keeps us ahead in the global competitive race is competence in certain skills, such as systems thinking and computers. I say *us* loosely, because it may or may not include *you* unless you have the skills and there are enough skilled people like you to meet a company's employment needs.

In this chapter we will review those skills which will give you an edge, both in your work and personal life. You can learn and refine a number of them, like English, second languages, and team building while still in high school. You can learn others in college, on the job, or by taking special courses. Companies spend millions of dollars sending their employees for training to develop skills that they can use at work, from listening skills and developing interpersonal relationships to systems thinking. As you'll read, there are lots of reasons for you to develop these skills, including the potential for solid financial gain and the pride of personal growth. We proceed.

Communication skills like English, English composition and literature and oral communications are the most critical to your success. Knowing how to read and understand what you read, and being skilled in reading research works will set you apart from the rest of your peers. Your ability to communicate your thoughts effectively can put you into positions of power and influence. Think about how exciting it will be to be recognized and admired for your abilities to accomplish things and to be sought out by others for your opinions. In financial terms, you'll have an edge in getting the best jobs available, earning thousands of dollars more than your peers. You'll get job offers because of your investment in learning these skills.

Skills in English are marketable in and of themselves. For example, a freelance professional editor for books can earn as much as $60 per hour. Authors of specialty books from children's stories to self-help books earn money both from the sales of their books and from public speaking engagements that often come as a result of their fame. How many movies have you seen that were adapted from current popular novels?

Fluency in *a second language* will open the door for opportunities you may not have thought about. Here's a real-life example. My son's friend applied for a job with a U.S. car manufacturer upon graduation from college. His grades were good enough to get him an interview, but his fluency in Japanese got him a job offer of $50,000 per year to start. He gets to travel to Asia three or four times a year on business, and he is constantly exposed to other great opportunities all the time — and he's only a few years older than you!

The population of Japan accounts for about 2.5% of the world's total population, yet look at the influence this nation has had on our globe. Imagine the impact you can have when you master the language and learn the culture.

When you think about second languages, it may help to know these facts: By 2015, the third largest ethnic group in California will be the whites. The Hispanic and Asian populations will be first and second, respectively. The Asian populations in Chicago and parts of Texas are so large as to significantly impact how employers hire and recruit managers.

The fastest growing markets in this hemisphere lie to our south and virtually all their populations speak Spanish. (One South American country's language is Portuguese. What country is it?).

Recently, I heard a terrific public speaker tell his audience that he was asked by an agent if he could do his presentation in Spanish, and answer questions from the audience in Spanish. He said he could not. The agent replied, "Too bad. If you could, I could get you $10,000 for an hours work."

Ni hui bu hui shuo Zhong Guo hua? If you are fluent in Chinese, you can communicate with 20% of the people in the world.

Learning to understand a country's culture as well as its language can enrich your personal life by exposing you to the joys of that culture. It is also fulfilling to feel the respect that others have for you because you understand them at a deeper level. The opportunities for employment and financial gain are a bonus.

Team building and collaboration, listening, interpersonal and conflict resolution skills deal with your abilities to get along with others and influence the results of your work together. Increasingly, we find that we can only get things done by working together with others whose individual strengths and talents are different from ours. In many schools, *teamwork* has resulted in students learning more material in greater depth together than individual students learn alone. In the work world, teams not only improve productivity, they also increase job satisfaction and employee morale. Simply put, people work better in groups, whether it is in school or at work.

Your abilities to bring people together, to get everyone to agree on what needs to be done and to do it, will serve you well not only in your work life. It will enhance your personal life as well. Your folks will be encouraged by the way you clarify with them what they want you to do. Your friends will appreciate the way you take the time to *listen*. You will feel great about the positive feedback you'll receive. Soft skills are the most powerful skills. Make a personal commitment to master them.

While great emphasis is placed on skills like listening, team building, and negotiating, none of these are answers in themselves. Academic skills, such as math, physics, chemistry, and biology are essential in your personal development. You'll need strong *analytical skills* in order to compete. Proficiency in math and physics are necessary for both aerospace engineers and video game creators. The person creating a *space invaders* game has to know almost as much about physics and math as an engineer on a real space mission. Getting together to build a space network or clean up the environment won't work if we are deficient in math and science skills.

Interviewing skills — is a combination of many skills, including thinking, planning, listening and socialization.

Many people think of interviewing as one sided, wherein one person asks all the questions and the other attempts to answer them with the intent of making a good impression and getting a job.

A good interview is actually an exercise in

which both try to get to know one another. Their mutual objective is to find out what they have in common and where they might differ, to see if there is a fit. In addition to sharing questions and answers, people also note each other's manners and personal behaviors. To many, a person's behavior style is as important as his knowledge or skills. Think back to the old expression, "You can dress him up, but you can't take him out."

Here is an example. A person was on an interview that went longer than expected, so his host invited him to lunch at a posh restaurant. Everything was going well until, at the end of the lunch, the prospect asked the waiter for a doggie bag for his leftovers. That one gesture cost him the job.

In preparing for an interview a person needs to look inside and ask questions like, "What kind of work excites me?" "What kind of environment do I want to work in?" "What skills do I bring to an employer?" "What are my attitudes?" This is not important just because the employer may ask exactly those questions. It is also important so you can assess whether the prospective employer is a fit for you.

You now know what millions of people don't—that the interview is as much for you as it is for an employer. By knowing what is important to you, you can weed out employment opportunities that don't fit you! In preparing for an interview, make a list of the questions an interviewer would ask. Then write down your personal answers to each question as an exercise in introspection and self-discovery. You'll be amazed at what you learn.

Systems thinking is a skill you may not fully understand. In its simplest definition it is looking for patterns of behaviors or functions. An example of systems thinking is an outbreak of an illness like legionnaires disease. The disease itself is caused by bacteria. The bacteria is transmitted often by the wind which carries it over a large area to unsuspecting people who inhale the bacteria. Some people get sick from the exposure. Others may die. They go to their local doctors and hospitals. The doctors and hospitals don't communicate with one another. The doctors treat their individual patients for the flu because the symptoms of legionnaire's disease are similar to the flu, and they see flu victims all the time. Since no one doctor sees all the patients, it is hard to pick up on a pattern in what's happening. It is only when we look beyond the individual patient's illness for a *pattern* that we discover the real illness. To see the pattern, we have to ask other doctors or hospitals twenty or thirty miles away if they are having a similar problem. Now you see how complex systems thinking can be, and how necessary systems thinking skills are.

You will experience many events in your lifetime that will seem isolated. With training you will learn to see the patterns and relationships. With training you'll become more adept at solving problems in the world once and for all. Here are some social problems that adults have not been able to solve that you and your peers might:

- Our environment is fast reaching the point where it won't be able to sustain the population growth. As we cut down forests to make way for civilization, we reduce the number of *oxygen generators* that provide the air we breathe.

Prisons are one of the fastest growing industries in the United States. What's wrong with this picture?

What can happen when hazardous waste gets into the groundwaters or permeates the atmosphere?

- Each year we dispose of billions of batteries from our radios, CDs and flashlights. Over time, the batteries decompose, leaking lithium, cadmium and other hazardous materials into our ground waters. What can or would you do about this? In your opinion, is it a problem at all? If it is, how will you get others to work with you to resolve it? What are the patterns?

- Prisons are one of the fastest growing industries in the United States. Currently, in Michigan, 1600 new inmates file into prison each week. Citizens pay almost $40,000 per inmate per year to keep them locked up while they spend about $5,000 per student per year on education, with marginal results. Most of the people locked up came from the lower socio-economic levels in our society. Are there patterns here? Has the problem been identified correctly? Is there a problem at all?

59

Systems thinking can make you rich. As you start to see patterns, you also see needs that you can take advantage of. Here are some current examples.

Two young men attending college in New York City needed money to pay their way. It struck them that as they listened to other students and visitors to the city that most people were lost. Many wanted to experience the best the city had to offer, but they didn't want to go off on their own and risk getting mugged. They were stymied. These two entrepreneurs set up walking tours of the city. They made so much money doing it that they added staff. At graduation time, one of the partners sold his interest and went off to pursue his other dreams, while the other is earning an excellent living helping tourists discover New York.

Opportunities are often disguised as problems.

Georges de Mestral wondered why burrs stuck to his trousers. He did some serious research to find the answer. He found that burrs were made up of thousands of hooks. After that discovery, he spent eight years trying to match the *technology*. The result was Velcro, which is now used in everything from clothes and shoes to the space shuttle.

Two college students of computer science who were looking for something to do created YAHOO, a directory and search engine for the internet. They became millionaires virtually overnight.

The point that I must stress is this. The world has always gone through changes. Each time, new industries replaced older industries. Farming once employed the majority of people. Today, it employs less than three percent of all workers. When automobiles achieved widespread use, buggy and buggy whip makers went out of business. They were replaced by assembly workers, gas station attendants and mechanics. Manufacturing, which today accounts for some 25 percent of U.S. workers, is in decline. Manufacturing in the next decade will account for as little as five percent of all workers. Industries like travel and tourism, telecommunications, home health care and other services are taking its place. Sharp, alert people — like you, perhaps — will make the discoveries that propel new and exciting industries into existence. To do this you must constantly prepare and remain ever vigilant. Life is full of exciting opportunities.

Organization Skills

You are probably already sensitive to the value of being organized, just from watching people who aren't. These people are always talking about having so much to do with so little time. They always seem to be stressed out and have little time for others. You don't have to be one of them.

> No yesterdays are ever wasted for those who give themselves to today.
>
> Brendan Francis

Learning *time management skills* means learning to prioritize your days, weeks, months and years — even your life. The key is to answer questions like "What is most important to me in my life?" and "What is the best use of my time right now?" If you have a term paper due in a month, it makes sense to work on parts of it over time until it's finished. Other people might have to cram the night before an exam. You know this causes undue stress. You studied the material over the weeks leading up to the test and will spend the evening before at the movies, relaxing.

> Live mindful of how brief your life is.
>
> Horace

Often times you'll find that there are a lot of things to be done, seemingly all at once. By prioritizing the tasks, you can put them in perspective and keep the stress to a minimum. Also, putting your plans on paper helps you to add things that are important, but often get overlooked, like time for yourself — and that's important. Planning (and taking) a vacation will give you the time to decompress and enjoy your life. If you forget to put a vacation in the plan, chances are you'll either never take one, or the one you take won't be as much fun as it could have been.

Organizing helps you eliminate wasted steps and allows you to get things done faster and with less stress. Organization skills include time management, but they also include things like how you plan your work and your *study habits*, how you layout your room and much more. Mastering one organizational skill, like time management, will lead you to work on and master others. The benefits to you include having all sorts of time you never knew you had and a major reduction in your stress levels. You'll understand just what that means to you when you look at all the harried people racing around, while you calmly and confidently go about your business. Life is better when you're organized.

Minutes are worth more than money. Spend them wisely.

Thomas P. Murphy

Problem identification and *problem solving skills* are excellent skills to develop and hone. They challenge you to always be curious, to ask *how* and *why* questions and to develop insights into things and events around you. While it might seem to you that this is not a real *job* because problems are easy to find, I can tell you that this is just not so. Most people avoid looking for problems. They'll say, "If it ain't broke, don't fix it." Many of them soon find out they've been replaced by the solutions. For example, years ago a person might have gotten angry enough waiting in line for credit card approval that she said, "forget it," and walked out. The manager of the customer service might have thought that was all right, because it does take time to process the information and sometimes people just don't have the time. Someone else thought, "That's a problem. How could it be fixed so people would never experience this hassle?" If you wanted to grow your business and make life easier for your customers and employees,

64

which person would you hire? If you were looking to start a career, which person would you want to be?

Manners

Manners are behaviors that demonstrate the respect one has for one's self and for others. Common courtesies like "Please" and "Thank You", the simple introducing of one's self to another or welcoming a stranger is almost a thing of the past. The application of common courtesies and simple table manners is a reflection of your upbringing and sensitivity to others. The lack of these simple, yet highly symbolic, social graces will limit a person's acceptance in society. Refining your manners will set you apart from others. You won't have to go far to see examples of this in your daily life. Commit to learn and use good manners consistently and constantly.

Personal Financial Planning

One of the biggest sources of personal stress for individuals and conflict in marriage today is financial distress. Stress is often brought about because people don't have the training necessary to prepare them for the financial realities of life. Frequently, young people fall into the trap of easy credit, only realizing their mistakes when they're well over their heads in debt.

There is every reason for you to invest your time to learn financial management and investment skills to help you avoid the pitfalls of mismanagement, to save and invest money for future uses, and to prepare for your retirement. It sounds silly, I know, to be talking about your retirement. But look around you at all the people that are retired and just scraping by. Be aware that the average fifty year old today has saved under $500 toward retirement. Is that the kind of lifestyle you want to live in your later years?

Would you like to have an easier life, free of financial worry? Investing in yourself and investing your money early are two ways to achieve that goal.

Here's an example I borrowed from a Public Broadcasting System (PBS) program called

The Wealthy Barber (see the recommended reading list). A person invests $5,000 every year for five years at 9%. He stops at this point, but leaves the money in savings. Five years later (ten years after the first investment), his brother starts investing, putting $5,000 each year into investments for twenty years, also at 9%. Who has more money at that point?

The answer is, the first one because he started earlier and the interest earned made his nest egg grow fast enough to make his smaller investment meet his retirement needs. The moral of the story is save early and often. It doesn't matter what the amount is as long as you get into the habit and stick with it. Don't be afraid to forego the most current model of some soon-to-be obsolete gadget. Look to the future! And don't overlook the reading list.

Action Steps   **If we were together, I would emphasize**

* Many of these skills can be learned and honed in high school. Use this opportunity wisely.

* Seek out training in the other skills.

Take summer classes or attend week-end seminars. Find books, video and audio tapes on the subjects you want to master. Have fun in the process.

* Stress levels increase with increasing responsibilities. Planning and solid follow-through will reduce much of it. Remember not to put off until tomorrow what you can do today (a lesson from Ben Franklin).

* Invest in learning stress management techniques from Yoga to meditation. Plenty of information is available.

* Commit to regular exercise and to eating right. Remember what Chris learned at a martial arts class — Discipline hurts less than regret.

Action Steps

5 — Competition You Will Face

Earlier we saw that the distribution of work by industry categories would be as follows: Manufacturing 5%, Services 91%, Agriculture 2% and Mining 2%. We also categorized jobs by company size. We said that only 15 % of jobs would be with large companies and 35 % with small to medium size companies. The rest, 50% of workers would be independents. Let's take a look at how people will compete for jobs under these conditions.

In large corporations, competition for jobs in the future will be more than just competing against others in the community or someone who is willing to transfer to the area. Competing for the future will mean competing against workers all over the world who are as well educated as you are — maybe better. A critical factor in this competition will be in the availability of enough skilled employees. Read through the following scenario:

HI-TEK is a global electronics company with headquarters in a nearby city. The company has research facilities in the United States,

France and India. It has manufacturing plants in the United States and India. HI-TEK is looking for a few researchers with specific qualifications to start a new project just miles from where you live. You have the right skills, but they need a total of thirty five qualified people and they can't find them. Most of the candidates from local colleges cannot communicate effectively, either in writing or orally. Senior management needs people who can keep them informed of the progress of their research and tell them what they need to do as research progresses. The company has a state of the art telecommunications network that links all their operations. HI-TEK facilities are linked electronically to one another, to their major customers and to their suppliers.

Ten years earlier, the government of India decided to make a commitment to invest in electronics technology as an industry for its people. This is similar to what the Japanese government had done for the automobile industry in the 1950's. The Indian government gave large grants to various universities in and around Bangalore. These grants allowed the universities to establish courses of study in computer science and to do research and development work in conjunction with leading companies in the electronics industry.

Graduates from local Indian universities are not only technically competent, they also possess well developed and refined communications skills. Because of their excellent communications skills (India is the second largest English speaking country in the world), strong technical capabilities and their proximity to leading Indian research universities, HI-TEK decides to connect them electronically to the home office and to fund a complete laboratory in India. The fact that the starting salary in India is $10,000 versus the $65,000 in the U.S. is not the issue. You didn't get the job because there weren't enough qualified people to support the project.

Today, many high-tech jobs are being done globally by employees living in different countries, with differing living standards, and at different rates of pay. A computer software writer in California earns $80,000 per year. His counterpart in France earns $35,000. His peer in India earns $10,000 per year. $10,000 seems like a substandard wage to us, but in India it's a very good wage. The average annual wage in India is $300 per year. The Indian employee is living quite well in his country. There, a custom-made suit sells for $20 and lunch for five at a trendy restaurant costs $10.

India is not the only country capable of supporting high tech industries with high quality local engineering talent. Singapore, the Philippines, Malaysia and Indonesia are also heavily competing for high tech industries. Each is getting a share.

Global companies are also investing in their employees. U.S. multinational companies are routinely educating their best engineers, via satellite, from U.S. universities. They beam college courses into their plants around the world. People globally are mastering the newest technologies. Naturally, the number of people qualified for the limited number of jobs will increase. Soon, salaries will become an issue that you will have to face.

Let's move now to the fifty percent of workers

who are self-employed. These workers range from knowledge workers to trades people. Knowledge workers are successful to the degree that the knowledge they have is in demand and the way they use it adds value. You can be an expert creator of buggy whips, but if no one wants them, the knowledge has no commercial value. But everyone likes to see a great movie, so proven directors are always in demand. They have special knowledge, *and* they know how to use it. Both characteristics are essential. If a director brings a story to the screen and it's a hit, he or she is successful and sought after. Have two or three *bombs* in a row and the phone stops ringing. The knowledge is still in demand, but not this director.

A skilled editor is sought after by authors or ad agencies. Consultants are in demand to the extent that they produce results for their clients. A good finish carpenter is seldom out of work.

Note that these people are also highly mobile. They can relocate either physically or electronically.

Who do these people compete with? Others like themselves. What sets them apart in their field are their individual skills, their personal creativity and their great reputations.

Earnings are largely a matter of the field they are in and the value they bring to their work. A hit movie will generate millions of dollars in profit; a great house, a few hundred thousand. Each person's contribution is a part of the end product. Each person's reward is a part of the success of that product. Competition for individual entrepreneurs depends on the size of the field and the number of qualified people in it. Carpenters outnumber directors.

Small to medium size companies are successful as long as they produce the results their customers demand, and do it at a profit. Small companies don't pay the wages or provide the generous benefit packages that large companies do. They just can't afford it. Where possible, small companies also use contract labor. Colleges are an example. Many private colleges use adjunct professors to teach part time. They are paid a flat fee for each course they teach. No benefits are included.

Small companies have to watch their expenses very closely if they are to survive. Profit often comes as a result of keeping costs low. In order for small companies to grow in sales and profits, they must do more work for their customers or add services for which the customer is willing to pay. Success in small business is always a challenge.

As an employee or an independent contractor, your challenge will be the same, to do something or make something that people want — better, cheaper and faster than anyone else. Success will be a challenge for you, too.

If we were together, I would emphasize   **Action Steps**

*   Invest and reinvest constantly.

*   Invest in your personal growth and development.

*   Invest your earnings for personal financial growth.

Action Steps

* Invest in your relationships with close friends, family, and loved ones.

* Establish and cultivate strong associations in business.

* Cherish and protect your reputation.

6 — Personal Issues

In this chapter, we will try to touch on a number of concerns you may have about yourself, high school and the world you will be entering when you leave it in just a few years. You are not the only one considering these issues, but you are one of only a small percentage of teens to get the answers.

Every time you are unsure why you are doing something, a yourself, WIIFM?, What's in it for me The answer will he you through even toughest course.

High school is much more than a place to prepare for a career. The main objective of a high school education is to prepare students to take their place in society as well-rounded, responsible citizens and contributing members of society. If it were not so, the curriculum could be limited to functional courses, notably science, engineering, English, computers, and vocational training. There would be no need for social studies, history, literature, art or second languages.

When you leave high school, you should have strong language, math, science and computer skills, an appreciation for the arts, an understanding of the underpinnings of our history and its relationship to why we are the way we are now. If you accomplish these objectives, you'll be well on your way to a successful life.

Your responsibility is to do your best to learn as much as you can about the wide variety of subjects you will take and to participate actively in the discussions of ideas and concepts that derive from the study, not just for yourself but for the contribution it makes to enhancing everyone's learning. Most of all, your responsibility is to yourself; it is not to your parents, not to your teachers, but to yourself! You don't want to look back years from now and say, "I should have." You should say, **I did!** ..

Here is a real-life story of someone who didn't have this advice.

Nancy was seething with rage when she arrived home. She slammed the door as she entered, alerting her husband and their children to beware. As she entered the kitchen, her husband asked, "How did the meeting with the principal go?"

"Terrible. And I never want to speak to my

parents again as long as I live."

"What have they got to do with your job interview?", he asked, obviously stunned.

"Everything. Their lousy parenting cost me the chance to teach."

"You've lost me, honey. Start at the beginning."

"Well, we were in the middle of the interview when Mr. Robertson, the principal, told me there was little chance that I'd be considered for a position. He said that, in the first place, public schools in the state usually hire people with a Masters degree. I don't have one. So I asked him if everyone had a masters, and he said no, and exceptions have been made in the past for the right candidate. He said I also would need a teaching certificate, and I told him I was studying for the test and hoped to take it next week. Then he said, 'Looking at your undergraduate performance, you graduated with a low *C* average. That's unacceptable in this state.' I couldn't believe it!"

"So what's this got to do with Mom and Dad?"

"Don't you get it? It's *their* fault. They should have told me this would happen. They should have been tougher on me in high school and college. If they had, I wouldn't be in this fix

Take your life into your own hands, and guess what happens? A terrible thing: no one to blame.

Erica Jong

today. They didn't say anything! Now I have to live with their mistakes."

When I first heard this story, I thought, "How immature can you get?" A grown woman, a college grad no less, mad at her parents because of her own marginal performance. I remembered what I was like as a teen, with my mother, a full-time working mom struggling to make ends meet, supporting three children. I know how many times she told me that a college degree was a must, though she had only made it through high school herself. I don't remember her saying anything about grade point averages, though. Maybe it was like that for Nancy. Like my mother, I am sure that Nancy's parents were doing the best they could. Perhaps *she* should have done *her* best.

Now that you've read this story, you know that you will never be able to blame your parents for your performance. You now know what is expected and who is responsible for your success.

I am responsible for my own well-being, my own happiness. The choices I make regarding my life directly influence the quality of my days

Kathleen Andrus

81

Your advantages

If what you have read has caused you to worry about your future, don't despair. Look at your advantages. First, if you're part of the target audience, you're a teen in high school or just starting college. The advantage is that you have *time* — time to define what is important to you, time to assess your strengths, time to learn and time to prepare. If you've been less than exemplary student, you also have the time to change your behaviors. Your second advantage is that you are in school, where many of the skills we've talked about are taught. You are surrounded by many learned people who committed their lives to helping you and others like you to succeed. Your third advantage is that there are many organizations that want to help you learn and prepare, from local businesses to the Rotary Club, which sponsors programs to help students. In many communities there are mentors who volunteer their time to help students find their paths. With all this time and support, all that is needed is your vision, your commitment and your persistence. If you are willing, there is a way for you to succeed.

The Role Your Teachers Play

Now let's think a moment about the teachers' roles in your development. The teachers' responsibilities include providing you with an environment that motivates and supports your learning, that challenges you to work outside of the assigned chapters and delve deeper into each topic for the personal rewards it gives; to connect his or her course of study with other courses you are taking.

Not all teachers can do this for all their students. Sometimes, they find themselves at odds with some students, even though they try to maintain a balance. You know, too, that not all students actively engage in the process of learning. They can even be a drain on the whole class. Still, in the course of your high school years you will have classes with some excellent teachers whom you know are your favorites. The contrast between your favorite teachers and other teachers is important to understand, so let's take a minute to make some distinctions.

Who are your favorite teachers? Why? While

you'll have to give them names and faces, I think I can tell you why they are your favorites. See if you agree or can add to this: your favorite teachers really cared for the subject they were teaching, and infused you with much of the same passion and joy for the subject. Your favorite teachers cared about you as an individual as well. Your teachers brought out the best in you and others and made learning fun.

As a result of being with great teachers you worked harder, studied longer, absorbed more, and got better grades than you got in other classes. And, even if your grade was not as high as you got in other classes, you knew it reflected what you deserved and considered it fair.

Now, what about your other classes? If you didn't like a subject or feel close to the teacher who taught it, how much did you pay attention in class? Did the class seem to go on forever? Did you apply yourself less to this course than to the others? There are some important lessons here for you.

Let me explain. Your relationships with your teachers are not much different than your future relationships will be with others in the *real world*. Many of the assignments you'll be given at work will be about as exciting as your most boring high school subject. Yet you'll be expected to work with others, including your boss to deliver a high quality result, on time. When you get to college or into the workplace, your success will in large part depend on what *you* do and no one else, just as Jack told me years ago. Your discipline and perseverance and desire to do well will determine how well you fare.

It doesn't really matter if your teacher is not the greatest or the subject is not high on your list. You get, in any given course, the teacher you're going to get. It is then up to you to decide what you want out of this course. Do you want an "A" or a "B", or will you take a "C" or "D," and then blame your poor grade on the teacher? You see, the teacher is not submitting your grades to the college of your choice, *You are!* The grades on your work don't reflect your teacher's performance. They reflect yours! You have a choice of what that grade will be. That choice is reflected in your behaviors. Are you going to do whatever it takes to keep the grade up? You should, because the grade has your name on it, the subject is important to your future. Most of all, it reflects your standards of what is acceptable to you. What do you want that standard to be?

In school, if you elect to do a marginal job, your grade will reflect your performance. In work, if you elect to do a marginal job, you may find yourself out of a job. Attitude is a very important element in the way you handle assignments. Always keep a positive attitude and, when the job is less than exciting, ask yourself how you can make it exciting and interesting. Then go ahead and make it fun. People who take on the tough, thankless tasks, and do them well earn a high measure of respect for their efforts and set themselves apart.

Everyone likes to be involved in things that are fun and interesting. One way to add fun to a course that is not fun is to put more of yourself into it. Remember how your best teachers put so much of themselves into a class that you were drawn into it? Well, why not do the same, in reverse. Get your peers to decide with you what would make the course more fun and then draw the teacher into it. Sounds crazy, doesn't it? But what if, by doing a little more research than the homework assignments called for, you developed questions, the answers to which you really wanted to know, and then posed them to the teacher? Or, what if you just demonstrated by the quality of your participation in class that yours was a better than average class and that the teacher would have to raise his level of contribution to keep up. The important thing is to realize that the quality of the learning is, in part, up to you. Wouldn't you really want to be part of the best class? Make it so.

Action Steps   **If we were together, I would emphasize**

* Not every teacher is a star. Not every boss or supervisor will be either.

* If you want something to be fun as well as productive, work to make it so.

* Learn early how to influence behaviors
  you want, so you can create the outcomes
  you deserve.

* Putting all your efforts into your classes is
  great training for your working life. Great
  habits yield great results.

The Parents' Roles

Your parents' roles in your high school education are a lot different than when you were in elementary school. In elementary, your parents worked with you to complement the teacher's work. At home, they might have worked with you on math, using addition and subtraction tables. They might also have helped you learn to read from the school books. By high school, you should be shouldering all the responsibility for you educational development yourself. No one should have to wake you in the morning or ask you in the evening if you've done your homework for the next day. That's your responsibility. It's part of maturing. It comes with the territory.

Speaking for myself, I couldn't help my sons with some of their homework, such as algebra or trigonometry because my skills were no longer up to the task. They had to rely on their teachers and their peers to help them. Getting help from the right source when you need it is also your responsibility.

By this point in your life, you have probably

arrived at the realization that your parents are flawed. You can cite chapter and verse the mistakes they have made — with one another, with their children — and with you. Your dad will never be Bill Clinton and your mom will never be Oprah Winfree. There may never be enough money, or vacations in sunny climates. And worse, there may never be the time to just talk, to share real insights, to build bridges and create lasting memories. But I must tell you this — they are doing the best they can — the best they know how.

I remember as a boy of thirteen looking out the window of my bedroom at the yard below. To the right, in the driveway, a Jeep had pulled in, and exiting from the passenger side, to my amazement was my father. It had been *years* since I had seen him. My younger brother and sister were racing to greet him. Vincent jumped into his arms as Cecilia embraced his left leg. I ran from my room. Down the stairs I flew, bolting to the door, awash in excitement and joy. I rounded the side of the house to....

I awoke with a start — perspiration enveloping me. I wanted that dream back. I wanted a happy ending. I was seventeen, old enough to realize all dreams don't come true. It took me another thirty years to make peace with my dad's flaws, to see him as a human being, just a man. In many ways he gave me gifts that I cherish still. He did the best he could. When I raised my children, there were many things I didn't know. But, from my experiences with my dad, I knew what *not* to do. I don't have those dreams any more. But I still love my father, for the gifts he gave, not for the things he couldn't give.

Ask your mom and dad about their journeys. What were some of the turning points in their lives? Let them tell the story their way. There's no need to point out mistakes. They will tell you where they made them and, because they love you, they will ask you not to repeat them. As you get older, you will notice that they are getting smarter.

Action Steps   **If we were together, I would emphasize**

* Sometimes people make mistakes just because they didn't know any better. They follow in the mold they know. Life is like that. Experience is what you make of it.

91

Yet, it doesn't have to be first hand experience. Learn from the mistakes of others.

* There is more information available and more support groups in existence today than at any other time in history. Ask for help if you need it.

* Give your folks all the help you can. Do your bit to show them you care. Pay more attention to your appearance, to your room. Pick up after yourself and do a chore or two without prompting. They can't help but notice the change. It signals maturity — and it may give you an opening— some time to grow together.

* When it's time, be the best parent you can be. No rush.

Learning From Others

Look closely at people who are older than you and have settled into their career and lifestyle paths. Try to determine:

How they are doing economically.
How much time they have for themselves, their spouses, and children.
The number of hours they work per week.
The number of jobs they have.
How much travel they do in their respective jobs.
How happy they are.
How happy their families are.
How they talk to one another, the amount of respect they show each family member.
Ask them to share with you their top five concerns.

Compare the people with the best mix of results (good job, salary, work schedule, time for family, friends, personal interests) to those with the worst mix (long hours, stressful working conditions, little time for anything else, few prospects for the future). Compare each person's level of vision, education, skills, attitudes and motivation. Draw your own conclusions.

Then ask yourself what you want in your future. Compare your own vision. Compare each person's level of vision, education, skills, attitudes and motivation to what you think you will need to achieve your desired results. Again, draw your own conclusions.

If we were together, I would emphasize   **Action Steps**

* Your future is just that - *yours!* It is up to you to decide what that future should look like.

* Your future success is a function of your commitment to make it happen.

* We all have choices to make - make yours wisely.

* Commit to do whatever it takes to achieve your dreams - then go for it.

* Only *action* yields results.

Heroes

Heroes have been with us always, though it seems that some eras have more heroes than others. There are very visible heroes, and there are heroes all around us that we don't see. Perhaps it is because of our individual definitions of heroism and what we call an heroic deed. In his book, *Heroes of My Time*, Pulitzer Prize-winning reporter Harrison E. Salisbury identified twenty people from around the globe whom he labeled as heroes from his 60 years with the New York Times. Here's an excerpt form his book's preface:

"These are men and women whose bravery burns in my mind and always will. They have stood alone and fearless in the face of danger and despair. We seldom see this quality in an age of packaged puffery, sound bites, and greed. My heroes blaze in the heavens like lightening on a dark summer evening."

One of Salisbury's heroes was Robert F. Kennedy, a man that Salisbury didn't like at first. Kennedy was hard driving, insensitive and focused solely on politics and winning. Bobby had all the answers. It was the change in Kennedy over a period of years that caused Salisbury to alter his view. The Bobby Kennedy that emerged after the assassination of his brother, President John F. Kennedy, was one who understood the finite nature of life, who was much more thoughtful, and who asked questions with humility. The Robert Kennedy who set his sights on the presidency in 1968 had the seasoning of time and experiences and, within him, the seeds of a great American president. Salisbury wept at the news of his death.

My heroes are closer to home and have lived within and influenced my existence. They include my mother, Dorothy, who held us together as a family even though she was estranged from her husband. When I graduated from high school, we didn't have the $1.75 between us to pay for my graduation picture. Yet she found the wherewithal to get three children through college. We never saw ourselves as poor though we were very often broke. Mother knew what she wanted for her children even if we weren't clear on that ourselves.

My heroes are my closest friends, Jack and Phyllis Osias, who befriended me with straight talk and personal dedication, and guided me through the tough years. They advise me still. They also started and ran the annual food drive for the needy in their surrounding communities for some twenty years, passing on the baton to younger hands when Jack reached his 80th year.

Who are your heroes? Why? These are not idle questions I am posing. You will do well to think about them in two ways. First, because your choice of heroes helps you clarify the values you admire and hold most dear. They may be personal courage or persistence, perhaps dedication, or the ability to persevere in the face of numerous obstacles. What qualities has your hero personified? Second, because these may be qualities you want to nurture in yourself. Whether you realize it or not, *you* are hero material, if only to the children you will work so hard to raise well or to the coworkers with whom you toil or do volunteer work. Your values will determine your value, to yourself and to society.

Your values will determine your behaviors and your actions, the work you do and the choice of associations you make.

Choose your heroes wisely. They are a reflection of you.

If we were together, I would emphasize

Action Steps

* If one of your heroes is a parent (or both), a teacher or someone close to you that is having a great impact on your life, tell him or her, or them. Heroes are people, too. Often your personal heroes don't know that they are. Your demonstration of sincere appreciation will raise their self-esteem, increase the strengths of your mutual bonds and bring you even closer together.

College is not for everyone

Of the top twenty fastest growing jobs as forecast by the Bureau of Labor Statistics, only six of the categories require a four year degree.(See appendix)

If you tell this to your parents, they might say, "Right on!" Or they may respond with "College is a must." The truth is that college is *not* for everyone, and the one to best decide whether college is a fit for you is *you*. But don't make this decision without serious investigation and thorough analysis. Historically, college grads have earned hundreds of thousands of dollars more than noncollege grads over their working careers. That in itself makes it worth considering. But you also have to consider your own leanings and the things you want to do with your life.

As in high school, the first years of the college curriculum are designed to expose you to a wide variety of topics, from art and the humanities, to music and literature, from second languages to history, religion, and government. The curriculum is designed to enlighten and challenge you, and to make you think in greater depth than you've ever done before. If none of this interests you, you'll probably be wasting your time — and lots of somebody's money.

Perhaps a better use of your time and energies is in vocational training in an area that you really like. There are good jobs available in the construction trades, like carpenters or plumbers — or in the kitchen as a chef. A chef who graduates from a reputable culinary institute can earn upwards of $80,000 to $100,000 per year. Most college grads don't come near those earnings. Good paying careers in electronics and computer often require vocational instruction and strong language skills. Humanities is not a prerequisite.

Consider an enlistment in the armed forces. The military has a lot to offer, including excellent vocational schools for those who qualify. Each branch offers scholarship programs, and each has programs for funding your college degree after you're discharged (see The Military Choice in the appendix).

If you're not sure whether or not college makes sense for you, make every effort to find out. Visit local colleges and universities, and experience college life for yourself, even if it's only a day. Talk to students at the campus

Colleges and universities will graduate 1.2 million people each year through 2005, each vying for the 850,000 available jobs. Every category, including lawyers, scientists, and managers is already filled to capacity.

Of the 147 million jobs in 2005, only about 21% will require a four year degree.

snack bar or the student union. Sit in on some classes. Observe how the students behave, how they interact with their professors and their peers. Ask the students what they're learning and the impact they feel college is having on their lives.

Find out how many hours students dedicate to studying to get the best grades. Inquire about the kinds of electronic media the college has and how easy it is to access. Get an idea of the number of computers the school has in the computer lab for student use.

Check out fraternities and sororities and other student activities that are active on campus. Students in these organizations are usually very active in college life and can give you valuable insights and guidance. Talk with the professors, too, especially those who teach subjects that interest you.

You'll be surprised how exciting a college environment can be. One thing you'll find out from the best students is that your results in college will be in line with your personal efforts. You're not a kid anymore.

Like many teens, college may be your first introduction to the concept of "freedom." No one will wake you up to get you off to class. You can cut one class, or all of them. If you and your friends agree, you can all party hardy all night, every night. Seemingly, no one cares if you even show up to class.

There's a good reason for this. The world needs mature, focused, hard working, dedicated, educated people. College is for responsible people, people who know why they're there and who are actively pursuing their personal goals.

The freshman year of college is as much a weeding out time as it is a learning time. The first year is a critical year for separating the sprinters from the marathoners. Your first exposure to college is possibly your first test of yourself, your goals, your self discipline, your assumptions, your persistence, your values, and your stamina. It is also your first exposure to an environment from which you can walk away. Think long and hard about this before you decide.

The Impact of Computers

It is impossible for me to overestimate the
revolutionary change wrought by computers
on our world, so I proceed with abandon.
No area of our life will be untouched by the
advent of the computer. Not education, not
work, not medicine, nor war; not travel, not
communication, not governments and
countries; not social structure. The computer
and its uses will be the great equalizer and
the great separator, purveyor of truths and
lies, the creator and the destroyer.

What we've seen is that we can wage war,
annihilating hundreds of thousands of foot
soldiers in desert sands, watching it live (and
sanitized) via television from literally
thousands of miles away.

What we've seen is that we can perform
medical miracles using computer graphics
and the analytical power of its computer
programming.

What we've seen is that we can design
products, simulate their performance testing,

and improve on them before the first one is produced.

What we've seen is that we can automate thousands of menial, labor-intensive jobs, and produce better quality goods more consistently.

What we've seen is that we can vastly improve the way we teach and the way we learn. Even tough subjects can be made fun to learn. In the process of learning, we can also enhance our desire to learn.

What we've seen is that we can separate ourselves from people around us, satisfying our ever growing need to feel safe and secure. Or, we can electronically reach out and bond with countless numbers of faceless beings who share views similar to ours — without ever having to meet them up close and personal.

In the final analysis, the liberating aspect of technology brings us to the concept of personal choice. We can choose to go inside ourselves and our homes — or we can choose to get out and be a part of the real world, and embrace the gifts of closeness and friendship. We can choose to contribute our thoughts and ideas without sharing a handshake or a hug. We can choose to communicate with anyone or no one. The nature and quality of our individual existence is up to us.

Life on the Web

Over 40 million people throughout the world use the world wide web for research, for business, for collaborating with others, for chatting, or for talking with special interest groups. Just about any type of information a student could want is available on the internet.

Connecting to the web is getting less and less expensive. Currently, connections are selling for as little as $15 per month for unlimited access, usually with a local phone number.

As a student, you can research the most difficult topics and create top quality reports for any class around the clock. You can find information that you need, download it to your computer, log off the web and proceed to prepare your assignment. With so much information at your fingertips, you may soon find the expectations of your professors have gone up. That's OK. It serves to make you a better student. Honest.

If we were together, I would emphasize   **Action Steps**

* Life is a journey, not a destination. Have fun along the way.

* Expand your imagination. Think far ahead, and anticipate the things that can happen. If something is positive, make a plan to participate in the joy of it. If something might be negative, plan how to neutralize it, prevent it from happening or how you will face up to it.

* Find time to share, to love, to grow and to give. You will never outgrow the need for sharing.

* Stay curious, inquisitive and open to new ideas.

* Stay younger longer.

7 — Creating your life

We have come to the end of our time together. I wish we had more. But I want to leave you with these thoughts from a father of two. What I've shared with you in this book can be viewed as a journey - your journey through your life. You will take this journey to its completion no matter what. How that journey unfolds and develops is largely up to you. You, until this point, may never have thought about this. Many people your age, hell, even older than I, never realize that truth. They mistake the end result for the journey. They say things like "Someday, I'll" or "Maybe, after.." They don't realize that the fun and the joy and the living is in the journey and that the end result may never be realized.

Achieving a goal is important, but it's the learning of new things, making valued friendships, experiencing life and having fun in the process that enriches your life. Knowing this early can enrich your life, so I give this to you as a gift.

I leave you with this thought, which I have

expressed many times earlier in the book. The most important thing to remember is that when you decide what it is that you want to be or achieve, that *no one* can keep you from it. Preparation is the key — preparation in the basics coupled with your personal faith that, while you can't yet see your own path clearly, when you find it, you'll be ready to walk it with ease and pride.

If we were together, I would emphasize   **Action Steps**

* Life is finite, yet full of joyous opportunities. Give serious thought to how you want your life to be, and determine how you can accomplish the results you desire.

* Develop a strong personal vision of what you want. Keep it always clear in your mind. Head for it like a beacon in the night. Understand that reaching your goal will always require periodic course corrections, and commit to remaining flexible.

Action Steps

* No matter what you decide, you must be willing to accept responsibility for achieving your goals unconditionally and regardless of the outcomes. If things go awry, look on the process as a learning experience. Make any necessary adjustments and move forward.

* Surround yourself with people who have similar goals, motivations and positive outlooks. They will understand your drive and ambitions and will make every effort to help you. Their successes will spur you on just as yours will serve to encourage them in their pursuits.

* Seek help when you need it, whether it is guidance, emotional support or financial assistance. Be willing to help others who come to you without expectation of personal gain.

* Always seek knowledge of many things. Try to find a balance between your work and the other elements of your being.

Action Steps (the final one, so fill it up)

Appendix

Fastest growing occupations

Fastest growing industries

Industries with largest job growth

Reasons to go to college

Reasons why *not* to go to college

Reasons why people chose the college they did

College credits through CLEP

External Degree Programs

Median starting salaries of college grads, 1993

The military option

Recommended reading list

Fastest Growing Occupations 1994-2005

(in percent)

Personal and home health care aides	119
Home health care aides	102
Systems analysts*	92
Computer engineers	90
Physical and corrective therapy aide	83
Electronic pagination systems workers	83
Occupational therapy assistants and aides	82
Physical therapists	80
Residential counselors	76
Human services workers	75
Occupational therapists	72
Manicurists	69
Medical assistant	59
Paralegals	58
Medical records technicians	56
Teachers, special education	53
Amusement and recreation attendants	52
Corrections officers	51
Operations research analysts	50
Guards	48

Over half of these occupations are in the health or social services areas

*Author's note: Only categories in **Bold** require four year college degrees. Requirements for the other categories range from on the job training to formal vocational training.

Source: Bureau of Labor Statistics, *Occupational Outlook Quarterly*, Fall 1995

Fastest Growing Industries 1994-2005

(in percent)

Home health care services *	120
Residential care *	83
Miscellaneous business services *	79
Automotive Services, except repair	75
Computer and data processing services *	70
Individual and miscellaneous social services *	69
Offices of other health practitioners	65
Child day care services	59
Personnel supply services *	58
Services to buildings *	58
Miscellaneous equipment rental and leasing	51
Security and commodity exchanges and services	50
Management and public relations	47
Nursing and personal care services	46
Health and allied services not elsewhere classified	46
Miscellaneous personal services	45
Miscellaneous amusement and recreational services	44
Job training and related services	43
Museums and botanical and zoological gardens	42
Motion picture production and distribution	40

A large number of these fast growing industries (*) also account for the largest numerical increase in jobs.

Source: Bureau of Labor Statistics, *Occupational Outlook Quarterly*, Fall 1995

Industries With the Largest Job Growth 1994-2005

(in thousands of jobs)

Education, public and private	2,213
Personnel supply services	1,310
Miscellaneous business services	1,077
Eating and drinking places	1,020
Nursing and personal care facilities	751
Home health care services	665
Computer and data processing services	661
Grocery stores	593
Offices of physicians	566
Individual and miscellaneous social services	536
Residential care	498
Services to buildings	496
Hospitals, public and private	485
Miscellaneous amusement and recreational services	429
Local government except education and hospitals	369
Legal services	343
Management and public relations	333
Child day care services	298
Hotels and other lodging places	282
Miscellaneous shopping goods stores	271

Top 8 will account for half the growth in wage and salary jobs. The top 20 will account for nearly 80 percent of the growth in wage and salary jobs. The Bureau of Labor Statistics projection models are made up of 260 industries.
Source: Bureau of Labor Statistics, *Occupational Outlook Quarterly*, Fall 1995

Reasons to Go to College

You want to

College grads earn more money during their working career (about $700,000) than those without college degrees*

College grads get better jobs

You really like the academic life

It is necessary to get into the field you want

You want the intellectual challenge

Your folks want you to

Everyone in your school goes on to college

You want the "college experience"

*Based on historical data. This may not hold true in the future.

Reasons *Not* to Go to College

You have no interest in academic subjects

Other interests are more important to you

You don't have the money

You're not ready to tackle the responsibilities

You want to get a job instead

You want to travel

Your parents want you to

Everybody in your school goes on to college

Vocational training is faster and more meaningful

You have more immediate concerns

It doesn't mesh with the way you see yourself

You are not prepared emotionally or mentally

Why People Chose the College They Did

It was close to home
It was *far* from home

It was what they could afford
They received a scholarship
The college had the best financial aid package

The school is a recognized leader in their chosen field
The curriculum met their educational needs
The school's reputation
To network with others
Status
To associate with the best and the brightest
They liked the challenging environment
Ratio of professors to students
Size of student body
Ratio of women to men

It was consistent with their self-image
Their closest friend was going there
Their parents went there

It is Ivy league

The environment is not too taxing
Entrance requirements were loose
It's a great party school
It has great sports teams
The climate suited them

College credits through CLEP

The College Level Examination Program (CLEP) was designed to help people shorten the time to get a degree by allowing them to *test out* of subjects they already know well enough to pass. For example, let's say you really like art and humanities and read a lot about them on your own. If you were given a comprehensive final exam on the broad elements of the subject, you are confident you would pass it. Then, the CLEP has a test for you.

You can sign up for a CLEP test at any local college that gives it (usually, any college will administer the tests once a month). The fee is somewhere in the range of $42 - $55. If you pass the test, you have earned college credit for the course (usually 3-4 credits, depending on the college). In effect you've reduced the time by some fifteen weeks and saved as much as $350 in the process.

To find out more, visit your local library or bookstore and ask for the books on the CLEP. The CLEP manual includes outlines of each type of course—Math, English, Economics, Humanities—and recommended readings to bring up your level of proficiency. It even includes sample exams for each subject, so you can test your current knowledge against the standards. If you get a score above 50 percent on the sample test, I would suggest you take the test.

External Degree Programs

You might think of these as colleges without walls, whereby it is up to you as the student to learn the subjects on your own, take the tests, and get the grades—all outside of a traditional college setting. External degree programs are great if you travel a lot, or relocate with a job and can't transfer your college credits to a college in the area. Understand that colleges are businesses, too, and they have restrictions on what they'll accept from outside schools.

Be wary of the college you choose. Make sure their degrees are accepted by major universities as the basis for your next degree. I know, for example, that a degree from Charter Oak State College, a State of Connecticut external degree program, is accepted at colleges all over the country, including Yale. Other programs have acceptance only within the school you're attending, so you are then "locked in" when you want to pursue a masters or a Ph.D. There is an excellent book listed in the appendix that lists 100 accredited colleges and universities titled *College Degrees by Mail*.

External degree programs may not be the right vehicle for you because you want the college experience and the benefits that come from it, including:

- The fun of being in an academic environment, where learning involves interacting with others, and being exposed to great teachers and exciting courses.

- Socializing with students from all over the world, with diverse backgrounds.

- Support throughout the academic system to sustain you when you feel like cutting out, and tutoring from peers for your most difficult subjects.

You can only get those experiences by being there.

Median starting salaries of 1993 graduates 1 yr. after graduation

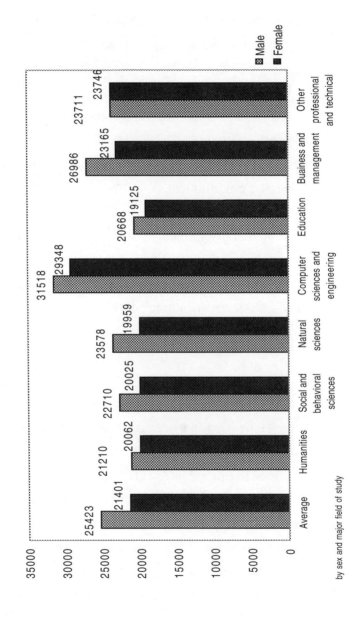

by sex and major field of study

The Military Option

There are many reasons for you to consider military service as a path after high school. Here are some:

- You want to serve your country.
- You see yourself as a leader and want to learn and develop leadership skills.
- You want to learn more about yourself by putting yourself in a challenging environment.
- You, like many people, like an ordered life. Military life is structured and disciplined. A soldier knows what is expected of him or her almost everyday of the enlistment.
- You would like to get a college degree but can't afford it.
- You want to learn vocational skills that you can use in civilian life.

There's a lot to be said for a tour of duty in the military after high school, especially if you are not sure what it is you want to be. There's the travel. The U.S. military has bases all over the world. Imagine being stationed in Europe or Asia for a year. You get to meet a lot of new people and experience new cultures. You can even learn a new language. With thirty days vacation per year, you can plan exciting trips to other countries. I have friends who were stationed in Italy, who spent parts of their vacations in France, Germany and the Swiss Alps. They loved it. Do you know how many years you will have to work in a civilian job before you get thirty days vacation a year? There's the opportunity for personal growth. The military is a great place to learn life skills like discipline, responsibility, and leadership. Soldiers and sailors who are not a lot older than you are entrusted with a great deal of responsibility. They are charged with protecting the bases on which they're stationed or the ships they're aboard. They are given responsibility for millions of dollars in sophisticated, high-tech equipment.

If you are the one who has earned this trust, imagine how highly this reflects on you. You grow up fast in the military because it is *assumed* that you have what it takes to do the job. Think about that! You're a teen, yet you are treated like an adult, part of a team that is recognized the world over.

The military offers a wide variety of training programs to meet its needs. They range from the construction trades — plumbing, carpentry, electrical, and heavy equipment operation — to mechanics, medical and dental technicians, to hotel and restaurant management. Many high-tech electronics, engineering and programs in scientific disciplines are available to those who qualify. There is even training for reporters and photographers. There are over 125 training programs. Many of the courses also qualify for college credits.

If you want to get a college degree, the military offers a number of ways to get one. If you take college courses in your spare time while on active duty, the military will pay 75 percent of the tuition costs.

You can take courses at a college campus or by mail. Either is acceptable.

Another option is to join the Reserve Officers Training Corps (ROTC). There are a number of variations of ROTC programs, but they all cover tuition and pay a small allowance. There are specific minimum requirements for acceptance in ROTC programs.

Yet another route is the Montgomery GI Bill. In this program, $100 is deducted from your pay each month for the first twelve months of your enlistment. You will be eligible to receive at least $10,800 in educational benefits. At the time of this writing, the amount is $14,400. You will be eligible to use your benefits after two continuous years on active duty. These benefits expire ten years after your release from active duty. There is even a plan for reservists, called Selective Reserve Duty, that pays over $7,000 for college expenses. Any recruiter in any branch of the armed forces can tell you more about these programs when you're ready.

With all the emphasis the military places on training and education, the following statements might not seem necessary, but I think they are. Our whole world is changing as a result of rapid leaps in technology, from lasers to medicine or fiber optics. The military is being impacted as well. In many cases, it is in the forefront of change. This means that the caliber of people they enlist has to be as high as any civilian job. High tech weaponry needs people of skill to operate it. The military is as demanding of its people as any quality civilian employer. Whether you're looking for a tour or a career, be prepared to contribute to the fullest.

Consider enlisting in the military for what it can do for you. It will challenge you to be your best. You'll have the chance to become a leader. The military will train you for jobs you can do in civilian life. It will fund all or most of your college education should you decide you want one. You'll learn and be able to apply the lessons of discipline, responsibility, accountability, and leadership. In just a few short years you'll have a lot of achievements for your resumé.

Employers look favorably on applicants who have had military service. They see them as candidates who have discipline and a strong work ethic. Employers also value the quality of training the military gives its soldiers and sailors. A stint in the service is far from a waste of time. It can be very valuable preparation for your future.

Recommended Reading List

Book	Author	ISBN#
Occupational Outlook Quarterly	Superintendent of Documents PO Box 371954 Pittsburgh, PA, 15250-7954	This is a subscription. Two years for $19
The Three Boxes of Life and How to Get Out of Them	Richard N. Bolles	0-913668-58-3
Do What You Love, the Money Will Follow	Marsha Sinetar	0-440-50610-1
Wishcraft - How to Get What You Really Want	Barbara Sher	345-34087-2
The Mainspring of Human Progress	Henry Grady Weaver	0-910614-02-4
Zen and the Art of Making A Living	Laurence G. Boldt	0-14-019469X

The Work of Nations	Robert B. Reich	0-679-73615-8
Asserting Yourself	Sharon Anthony & Gordon H.Bower	0-201-57088-2
A Peacock in the Land of Penguins	Barbara Huteley Warren H. Schmidt	1-881052-71-0
Smart Questions	Dorothy Leeds	0-425-11132-6
Listening, the Forgotten Skill	Madelyn Burley- Allen	0-471-08776-9
Creative Visualization	Shakti Gawain	0-553-22689-4
Choices	Shad Helmstetter	0-671-67419-6
Finding the Fountain of Youth Inside Yourself	Shad Helmstetter	0-671-74620-0
The Art of Talking So That People Will Listen	Paul W. Swets	0-13047-837-7

How to Write and Give a Speech	Joan Detz	0-312-08218-5
Presentations Plus	David A. Peoples	0-471-63103-5
Doing it Now	Edwin C. Bliss	0-553-27875-4
Study for Success	Meredith D. Gall, Ph. D	0-9305-3901-4
Skills for Success	Soundview Executive Book Summaries 5 Main St. Bristol, VT 05443	
How to Get Your Point Across in 30 Seconds or Less	Milo O. Frank	0-671-72752-4
The Wealthy Barber	David Chilton	0-7615-0166-5
Looking Beyond the Ivy League - Finding the College That's Right for You	Lauren Pope	0-14-02.39529
College Degrees by Mail	Bear & Bear	No ISBN# listed

The Index of	William J. Bennett	0-671-88326-7
Leading Cultural		
Indicators		

The Rubicon Dictionary	John Cook	0-9630359-3-2
of Positive, Motivational		
Life-Affirming &		
Inspirational Quotations		

The Lessons of	Will & Ariel Durant	Library of
History		Congress #
		68-19949

I have included ISBN #s or Library of Congress numbers for you because it is sometimes easier for a book store clerk to access a book using them instead of the name.

Order Form

Imagine the Future - A Teenager's Guide to the
        Next Century - and Beyond _____copies
Imagine the Future - A Parents' Guide   _____copies

                 _____ total

1-99	_____ copies @	\$8.95	each = \$_____	total
100-999	_____ copies @	8.25	each = \$_____	total
1,000-4,999	_____ copies @	7.25	each = \$_____	total
5,000-9,999	_____ copies @	6.25	each = \$_____	total
10,000 or more	_____ copies @	4.95	each = \$_____	total

PLEASE SPECIFY WHICH BOOK(S) YOU WANT AND THE RESPECTIVE QUANTITIES

Name _____

Title_____

Organization_____

Street Address_____

City _____ State_____ ZIP_____

Phone( )_____ FAX ( )_____

Purchase Order#_____(if applicable)

Check enclosed _____

Charge Account _____ Master Card ____VISA

ACCOUNT NUMBER _____ EXP. _____

SIGNATURE_____

Applicable sales tax, shipping, and handling charges will be added. Prices effective March 1997 are subject to change. Orders payable in U.S. Dollars. Orders less than \$100 require prepayment. \$100 or more may be invoiced.

Career Solutions

P.O. Box 99455 Troy, MI 48089-9455 (810) 879-0681 FAX(810) 879-6936

Yes,

_____ Please send me information on Imagine the Future seminars for teens.

_____ Please send me information on training programs for teachers and administrators.

Name _____ Title _____
Address _____
City _____ State ____ ZIP _____

Specifically , I would like information on :

_____
_____
_____
_____
_____

Mail orders or inquiries to

Career Solutions   P.O. Box 99455   Troy, MI 48099-9455
Phone: (810) 879-0681 Fax: (810) 879-6936
e-mail: jmalgeri@detroit.freenet.org

Feel free to call, Fax or e-mail us with your thoughts, concerns or things you're doing that are working/not working. We'd love to hear from you.